The Fucks That I Give

Joseph Stublick

BookLeaf Publishing

India | USA | UK

Presentation by *BookLeaf Publishing*

Web: www.bookleafpub.com

E-mail: info@bookleafpub.com

ISBN: 9789358317336

First edition 2023

For Liam.

ACKNOWLEDGEMENT

Firstly, I'd like to thank my mother and father. They've encouraged me to express my creative side for as long as I can remember. They've also given more fucks about me than any other two people on the planet. My sister, Molly, who is one of the most talented people I know, and the best friend I will ever have. All of my friends, Vibe Tribe, the Bradstock Art Resource Team and the rest of my FAMILY... There are so many of you. I am inspired by all of you every day, and I am so lucky to have every single one of you in my life. I fucking love you all, and I give more fucks about you guys than you could ever imagine.

PREFACE

We all as human beings can only give so many fucks. We can't fucking help it. Our energy can only be spread so thin. The problem is most of us throw our fucks all over the place and it drives us insane.

What you are about to find in this book is a small collection of song lyrics and poems I've been quietly (and sometimes not so quietly) writing and compiling for the last twenty years. Nothing super crazy. Just thoughts that have helped me continue to grow into who I am meant to be, and moments that helped me figure out the who's and what's I actually give a fuck about.

As you read through these pages, I encourage you to think about the people and things you have given your fucks to. Sometimes they're going to the right places. Sometimes they're not...

Maybe you don't give a fuck. Maybe you do. I leave that in your hands. The choice is up to you... I hope you enjoy.

Snow Song

I've been sitting here perfectly still
I'm spinning all around, I'm upside down
Secrets will be whispered just to keep from
going stale
This enchanted forest is perfectly designed just
for me and you

You and me, together we'll break down the
world
You and me, together we'll take on the world

Still I'm craving this hell, I'm spinning upside
down
I'm inside out
Secrets that I've whispered
They've shown there faces and those ugly places
Disenchant this forest
Its burning down now
It's dragging me down

I don't know but if you ask me one thing I'll tell
you that I do not have one God damn clue
But I can still remember all you've told me
From that I'll breathe

I am finally free

Dance With Me

Put a little faith back into the juke box baby
Put a little hope back into your heart
I don't know you
I can feel you
I promise I will never let you fall away
I promise I will never let you down

Darlin', Darlin', can't you see?
I've always loved you more than life
Darlin', Darlin', wont you please?
Let me feel your hand in mine

Cross your fingers a little longer
I'll burn alive to make you warmer
I know I'm not there yet
But I know I'm in your heart
I promise I will never let you fall away
I promise I will never let you down

Been living with a blindfold on 'till the day I met
you
Let me breath you in my dear
And give you all that I know
I'm closer than I've ever been to Heaven
Standing with you

Just let me breathe you in my dear
We've got nothing to lose

Darlin', Darlin', can't you see?
I've always loved you more than life
Darlin', Darlin', wont you please?
Let me feel your hand in mine

Her Skin

She's drunk on turpentine and arsenic
Just another night she can't forget
The taste of him still on her lips
The heat of his breath still on her skin

The stains of time still haunt her mind
Cigarette smoke wont cover his smell
The bruises gone, her pain wont fade
The weight of his words gripping her skin

Let me take you away
I know what you're searching for
Tell me not where your pain comes from
Cause I know, I know

She cries so much it hurts her soul
She tried to run she can't escape
The echos ring, her bones are cold
She cant even breath, its burning her skin

His piercing eyes…
Her heart explodes
Those bleeding tears…
Still cover her skin
Her skin...

Let me take you away
I know what you're searching for
Tell me not where your pain comes from
Cause I know, I know

Fun Gus

One day I came alive
I want to share this new perspective with the
whole world
She is at my fingertips
He lives within my fingerprint
As soon as I want him to, she becomes, he
becomes you

Then one night I started dancing
I want to share this microverse with the whole
world
Another day I started crying
I want to share my tears and my hurt with the
whole world

Too much Fun Gus in a day they say
Can have an adverse impact
On the surrounding stander buyers
God is in this chocolate chip

Can't you see this? I wish you could see this
Transcend my mind
These walls, they are breathing
Pupils dilating
The flower of life's been whispering

I'm in your mind

One more day we started laughing
Can't we share all our hope and this love with
the whole world?
Another day I started crying
I want to share my tears and my hurt with the
whole world
And then one day I kept on dancing
I want to share this macro dose with the whole
world
Our whole world

Dichotomy

Impact...

What happened?
I close my eyes to block out the sound
But it rips through and I shatter anyway
My chest burns and collapses
I can't even spit
I emerge destroyed

Pain...

You people bother me but I'm in no position to
be rude
You're generous
I'm irate
My mind closes but this feeling pries its way in
I love you
Close my eyes
I can see you watching me

Denial...

The situation strangles me
I give in to the opposition
I hear you

I close myself but leave the key
How did they find it?
I separate myself then cry

Morphine...

So this is the place everyone talks about
OK. Fine I'll melt
Sure, I can deal with that

Revenge...

I have no one
I cant move
I'll give this all to you
You have no face to me
I hope you suffocate with pain
You cry, I wont let you die
Don't ask
Ill never tell you
Slice your throat then fall
Torture would be generous
Relax
You're faceless
I am alive

Polish Lullaby

She don't want to be the only one
Who thinks the world is lost and gone
Seen so many things she don't want to see
But she sees them over and over again

I saw her just the other day painting in between
the stars
And all there was to see is the sad and the
sorrow hidden behind her eyes

All I wanted to do is walk up and say to you
Sit back, relax
I promise everything will be alright
All I wanted to do is walk up and say to you
Sit back, relax
Oh I promise I'll sing a lullaby

Saving a little but I don't really think so
Thinking I want to, but I don't really got to
But I will, yes I will
Looking for a cover with a little more color
But all you ever find is a little more trouble
And a little more, and little more

All I wanted to do is walk up and say to you

Sit back, relax
I promise everything will be alright
All I wanted to do is walk up and say to you
Sit back, relax
Oh I promise I'll sing a lullaby

Tommy Tsunami

Hey there mister
Can you tell me where you're going?
I don't think we should be down here but I'll let
you out
I want you to know just how real I can be

And I will tell them that you can give me what
I've been looking for
And I will burn them if you can give me what
I've been looking for

So now sister
I can tell you what my secret is
My mind is black and blue
My soul, bleeding for some time

How did you and I completely erase this empty
place?
How did you and I completely replace this
empty space?

I don't know you
You don't know my face
I will find you
And when I do I will get what I came for

Bad Things And Beautiful Women

Where are you going girl?
I want in
Its cold, dark, black & blue and pale... And you
cant win
What are you doing girl?
Show me how
I wont let you stop girl
Where do you rock?
Where do you drop?
Grind me all night long

I wont let you stay with me girl
Don't stay with me
This will be the last time I fall down
This will be the first time I stand up
So little angel wont you stay?
I will clip your wings another day

Back this up to the darker sides of my mind
I don't think you want to know where I have
been
Thorns they're digging deeper in through my
skin
I will tear every wall down that you've built

I wont let you stay with me girl
Don't stay with me
This will be the last time I fall down
This will be the first time I stand up
So little angel wont you stay?
I will clip your wings another day

Down On Me

Buenas noches, bonjoura seniorita
May I? Can I? May you go down, down
Down on me
Open up your eyes
Take a look all around you
Open up your eyes
Take one look up, oh wow no
In front of you

You're out of your mind and that does not
change a thing
I'll sing you this song until the sun comes up
I'll run my way out as easy as I came
And you will never see me again

Buenas dias aloha mademoiselle I say
Say, "eye?" Can I? May you go down, down
Down, down, down…
Take a hold of my breath and then I lock with
you
Rock with you, lock with you
To down town, down, down, down

Open up your eyes
Take a look all around you

Open up your eyes
Take one look right up, oh wow no
In front of you

Wisdom Tooth

I'm so tired of chasing my tale
I'm so tired of looking life right in the eye as I
say all I do
But these lies no longer work on me
It's time for you to find a new fool

Don't fall away
I'm a little tired of playing
But I will never wish this away
Every way I slide I'm dead
Turn around, pick me up, bring me back

You're eyes are burning holes through my skull
These lights are making me shake
But I wont let it break me down
Don't ever let me break you down
Its time for you to find a new fool

You fucking tool...

Stay

If only you would stay
I'd buy you flowers every day
If only you would stay
I'd show you love in infinite ways

If only you would not leave
I'd make sure that you believe
I'm everything you wanted
There's nothing to bereave

If only I could just rewind
I'd be more loving, and much more kind
I'd turn God's hands back to a time
When you didn't know the "me," that does not
shine

I'd make sure you never saw him
I'd be less angry, and much less grim
I'd be much stronger, and never weak
There'd be no evil about me
For you to speak

I'd shower you with love
I've got so much left to show
I'd make you the happiest woman alive

If only you would not go...

I haven't learned one lesson
Actually quite a few
But of all to me the thing that's most
important…
Is simply...

You

Rock And A Wet Place

Left for The Springs
To visit a friend
Nothing left, the world was dead
Begging this chapter to finally end

Got on a plane
Ran away to forget
All my dumb gambles
Choke my regrets

Floating through the gorge
I set my soul free
Finally a place I wanted to be
Finally peace as far as I can see

Stuck on a rock
On top of a fall
Friend, what happened next
I'm lucky to recall

Caught the rope
Thought I was good
But the current swept me
I jumped as far as I could

I couldn't breathe
I felt my heart race
It's a shitty feeling
Between a rock and a wet place

My hands were numb
My lungs were on fire
Life leaving my being
My body grew tired

How I kept going?
I don't really know
I had one choice
And that was, 'DON'T FUCKING LET GO!'

I screamed without screaming
I dug as deep as I could
I promised to change
If only God would

I broke through the surface
Drowning with fright
Sucked air in my lungs
And regained my might

Another rope?
You've got to be kidding me
Where is my peace?
I thought I was free

I caught it again!
How I did, I do not know
Round two bitch
Let's fucking go!

I reminded myself
I am alive
I want to go on
I want to strive

Had a conversation
With our good friend, The Lord
Then I surrendered
I laid as flat as a board

His hands wrapped around me
He pulled me ashore
Going limp, I heard a whisper
'You're finally free, so go and live more…'

Michael's Song

Every day it feels no different
Every note I draw feels the same
Every color that I breathe in
Makes me wonder where you've been

I'm afraid you wont hear me...

Show me a world with Lennon, no Chapman
Show me a world with Cobain, no shotgun
Show me a world where no one dies
Show me a world where no one cries

Every day we wake up without you
Every night I hear my mother cry
Every color that we all breathe in
Makes us wonder when we'll see you again

But we'll sing this song for your soul...

There's so much I would like to say
But I cannot, I don't think I'll get there
So many places I want to go
But I cannot, my tongue is tied

But I'll sing this song for your soul...

Show me a world where you're still here
Show me a world where I can still tell you
You light up all of our lives
And I don't ever want to say goodbye...

When This Guy Falls

This current hasn't been taking me
Where I wished it could but that's ok
Cause I'm kind of tired
And I think I lost my paddle about two months
ago

This current hasn't been taking me
Where I wished it would but that's ok
Cause I'm kind of tired
And I think I lost my paddle about three months
ago

It's ok...

I'll just close my eyes and fall asleep and then I'll
dream about all the places I'm gonna go but not
quite know until I'm there
And all the while I put my trust
In this here current I can't control

Take a deep breath and then exhale
I'm a little scared now but that's ok
Cause I'm falling asleep now
And I think I lost my paddle about five months
back

The air is thick and my hands are cold
I don't know where I'm going but that's ok
Cause I'm kind of tired
And I think I lost my paddle about six months
ago

But it's ok

I'll just close my eyes and fall asleep and then I'll
dream about all the places I'm gonna go but not
quite know until I'm there
And all the while I put my trust
In this here current I can't control

James

In spite of me, in spite of you
The biggest asshole we ever knew
For some strange reason
We all still loved you

Ignorant king of your tiny hell
Pretending to be well
You could have excelled
You were in so much pain, we all could tell

No control
Always in charge
Always insisting
You're living so large

Smarter than everyone
Stubborn to no end
The sorest loser and the loudest winner
Didn't know how to cook yourself dinner

I know I'm talking shit
But you just couldn't quit
I'll never forget when you called Molly a whore
I cracked you in the jaw and we threw you out
the door

You took everything for you
Everything in excess
It was finally time
For your soul to rest

In spite of this, I hope you're at peace
I hope you're free
We all still love you
In spite of us, in spite of me...

Fucked Up Again

I always say I'm gonna quit but I never do
I always say this will be my last sip but it never
is
That dumbass cop
He pulled me over on the parkway on a Tuesday
Way to drunk to get out the smart way

I fucked up again

I always feel like I'm gonna win but I never do
I could have fixed it, I had the chance, but I had
no clue
That dumbass cop
He caught me drinking at a casino with all my
bros
Nineteen years old, smoke in my pocket
Never had a chance to drop it

I fucked up again

I always said I was gonna change but I stayed
the same
I did it proudly, no one forced me, only me to
blame
I could have stopped

We were done before we said, "I do."
Tried as hard as I thought was right
Couldn't see things through

I fucked up again

Open fire before I take aim
So damn sick of this stupid game
I fucked up again
I'm lost without a paddle
But when I fall I hop back in the saddle
Find my balance, and ride back to battle

Then I just try not to fuck up again…

Four, Oh Five!

Box yourself out
Grab yourself the bar
Time to show yourself
Who you really are

One thirty-five
Two twenty-five
Remind yourself
You are alive

Straighten your spine
Three deep breaths
You're going to do this
With nothing left

Load four plates up
Skip three fifteen
It's time for four, oh five!
You know what I mean?

Grip it, and rip it! You know you can do it!
No one helping, no one around
Set your posture
Pull it off the ground

Your knees begin to buckle
Like old broken gears
You think you might drop it
You ignore your fears

You stand up tall
You pull yourself through
Four hundred five pounds
This feeling is new

You finally did it
Eleven long years
If they only knew
The blood, sweat and tears

The only who know
Are the ones who have won it
And I'm a member of that club now
I've finally done it

The Fucks That I Give

Typical cold
The sixteenth of February
This particular day
It was far from ordinary

I thought I had failed
I fell off the wave
It was the biggest fuck
I ever gave

I surrendered my life
My soul's been sucked dry
Keep giving it more
At times I don't know why

Haven't laughed in a while
I barely live
But this is my love
The fuck that I give

Life is what happens
While you make other plans
I wanted to be a creator
But became a sound man

I've grown sick and tired
Do you know what I mean?
Giving a fuck
About other people's dreams

With so little left
I keep feeding the fire
Dad said I can do it
If I have a burning desire

I'll remember the blood
All the tears that I've lived
'Cause these are the fucks
That I will always give…

www.ingramcontent.com/pod-product-compliance
Lightning Source LLC
Chambersburg PA
CBHW071233140726
47996CB00007B/2587